Pamplo Iruña

Editorial Everest would like to thank you for purchasing this book. It has been created by an extensive and complete publishing team made up of photographers, illustrators and authors specialised in the field of tourism, together with our modern cartography department. Everest guarantees that the contents of this work were completely up to date at the time of going to press, and we would like to invite you to send us any information that helps us to improve our publications, so that we may always offer QUALITY TOURISM.

QUALITY
TOURISM
WITH
EVEREST

Please send your comments to:
Editorial Everest. Dpto. de Turismo
Apartado 339 – 24080 León (Spain)
Or e-mail them to us at turismo@everest.es

Editorial director: Raquel López Varela

Editorial co-ordinator: María Dolores Crispín

Layout: Gerardo Rodera

Text: Antonio Iturralde

Photography: José Luis Carrión, Enrique Pimoulier, Santi Yániz and Archivo Everest

Cover design: Alfredo Anievas

Digital image work: David Aller y Ángel Rodríguez

Translation into English: Rebecca Ivatts

Cartography: © EVEREST

© EDITORIAL EVEREST, S. A.
Carretera León-La Coruña, km 5 – LEÓN
ISBN: 84-241-0195-2
Legal deposit: LE. 1.092-2006
Printed in Spain

EDITORIAL EVERGRÁFICAS, S. L.
Carretera León-La Coruña, km 5
LEÓN (España)

www.everest.es
General enquires: 902 123 400

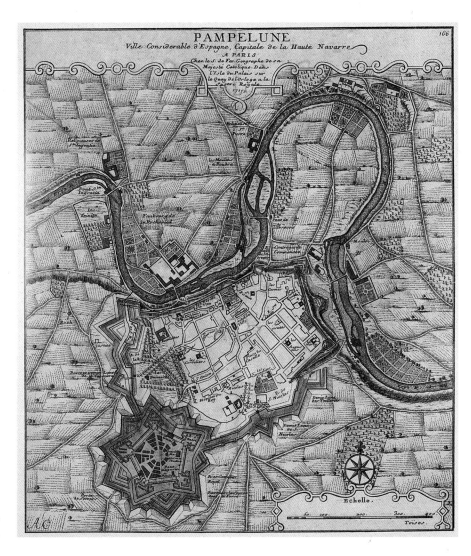

*Old map of the city
of Pamplona.*

HISTORY

Pamplona may have been around for 3,000 years but it still feels young at heart. The city started life as *Iruña*, a village inhabited by several hardy, combative Basques who established a small community on top of the hill. Pamplona has always occupied a relatively elevated position, but its 443,80 metres above Cantabria's sea level are reason enough to consider itself a high altitude city.

Pamplona was also home to people of Celtic origins – and no doubt there are other races, creeds and colours which will one day inhabit our lands. In 75 AD, a Roman gentleman – the General Pompey – arrived who would radically change the city's history and have a decisive influence on its future. The name given to this hill-top community was subject to the first big change; it went from being Iruña to the Roman title of *Pompaelo*, and its new inhabitants were mainly troops from the Roman Empire. Some say that it had become nothing more than a military camp, but others beg to differ.

In the first few centuries AD there were fires which virtually destroyed everything in their path, but from the ashes we, the inhabitants of Pamplona, rebuilt our homes and fortifications. The Visigoths and the Muslims occupied our lands between the 6th and 9th centuries and it was not until 905 AD that we had a king in Pamplona: Sancho Garcés I. His kingdom, together with the episcopal lands we had acquired in 589, constituted an independent kingdom: the kingdom of *Pamplona*.

Still under the vigilance of the Arabs we suffered a few skirmishes and Abd-al-Rahman III destroyed the city in 924.

Pamplona's historic centre and San Cernin church (pictured above).
San Nicolás church (right-hand page).

Barely one hundred individuals lived on mount Navarrería but we managed to remain fortified. In about 1100, people from the south of France began to arrive in the camps situated to the west; they were traders and craftsmen. They were devoted to the saint, **San Cernin**, to whom they dedicated the church and the name of the new borough: *Burgo de San Cernin.*

Attracted by the affluent lifestyle of these traders, people soon began to arrive from elsewhere; when they were not able to settle in Burgo de San Cernin or Navarrería, they created another settlement to the west which they dedicated to Saint Nicholas, and went on to name *Burgo de San Nicolás.* These three *burgos* (boroughs) soon became involved in quarrels and conflicts, and only on September 8, 1423 did Carlos III *the Noble* manage to reconcile such sworn enemies and unite the three walled and independent boroughs, by means of the «Privilege of the Union» treaty, creating one single city. We would now go back to being one city: Pamplona. After a peaceful situation was reached between the three boroughs, it was decided that La Jurería, the residence of the governors and the mayor, should be built on neutral territory, next to the Galea tower (also known as Portalpea) which stands where the fortifications of the three boroughs converge.

The conquest of Navarre and its incorporation into Castile in 1512 meant that we became a border town, and so our main concern was to build fortifications and walls to defend the border with France. We can now say that it was thanks to this difficult situation that in 1571 building began on the beautiful fortified Ciudadela (citadel) which, with a wall to the south and west, completed the total enclosure of our fortifications. We would later open the city gates of Francia (France), Rochapea, Tejería, San Nicolás y Taconera. The building of city gates culminated in 1680 with the opening of the *Portal Nuevo* (New Gate).

Aerial view of the Ciudadela.

From 1750 onwards, the city became engaged in a constant process of modernization and new buildings and structures were erected with new financial endowments. So we acquired a new town hall, a new neo-classical facade for the gothic Cathedral, a new sewage system, fountains across the city, and so on. But our modernization was abruptly interrupted by the French invasion: the only occasion in which the Ciudadela was seized was in 1808, when Napoleon's troops set up camp close to the fortress when they were denied permission to enter. Every morning a group of soldiers would come up to receive the bread rations allotted to the troops. On February 16, this same group came up while they were having a snowball fight. This trick allowed them to disarm the guards and let the rest of the troops enter.

The 19th century was one of upheaval for the city; from the cruel Carlist Wars in which we took the side of the liberals, to the people's *gamazada*. This was the popular protest against the attempt by central government and the Chancellor of the Exchequer, Gamazo, to reduce our financial autonomy. In commemoration of this protest, and as a symbolic way of honouring the city's fiercely independent spirit, the Monumento a los Fueros was built, and became Pamplona's iconic landmark.

In the same century our first local newspaper was published and the proliferation of illustrious figures in different fields gave rise to an intellectual movement of sorts. Amongst the musicians that excelled in their field were Sarasate, Gayarre, Gaztambide, Hilarión Eslava, Guelbenzu, Larregla, Astráin... And on the literary side of the fence, writers such as Iturralde y Suit and Campión were highly popular.

All that remains to mention is the city today, the developments of the 20th century and the urban and demographic explosion which we have undergone: the city has broken the straitjacket of its city walls and expanded to the south. But this urban explosion has also been technological, social and cultural. The fact that we now boast two universities bears witness to this. The industrial estates, – call them modern city walls if you will –, surround and sometimes block the urban expansion, but they have afforded Pamplona one of the highest standards of living among Spanish cities.

Iruña's original population of barely 100 individuals has now grown to almost 200,000; and of course this figure increases if we include the neighbouring populations of Barañain, Burlada, Cizur, Noain, and so on.

On these two pages, the Monumento a los Fueros (right) and the Salón del Trono in Navarre Palace (below).

A STROLL THROUGH THE CITY

After surviving so many attacks, and being subject to so much destruction and upheaval, the city of Pamplona is naturally friendly and receptive to visitors. As for the locals, we may seem abrupt and almost standoffish on first meeting but, once you get to know us better, you'll see that we're generally affectionate and helpful.

We invite all those who come, whether for a few hours or several days, to wander through the city, stroll along our streets and through our parks, visit our historical buildings, and see the city which with all its scars, renovations and new buildings, relates a real story which could not be told in words. Come and see for yourself.

Like every city in the world, Pamplona has a host of different facets, and boasts more than one environment worthy of admiration. Of course, according to the area of the city we're in, these environments bring different concepts to mind.

Identity

The greatest existing expression of Pamplona's identity is the **Plaza del Castillo**, a perfect meeting point for any new visitor. From here you can immerse yourself in the streets of the *casco viejo* (historic centre of the city), which is actually the union of the three original *burgos*, or boroughs, into which the ancient settlement, Iruña was divided.

Plaza del Castillo, yesterday (right) and today (below).

Architectural details from the Plaza del Castillo and the interior of Café Iruña.

This is Pamplona's real city centre, which when you're travelling by car, you see signposted as «*centro ciudad*» and never know quite when it's going to appear. This is not the exact geographical centre but rather the heart of the city. Here, is where bull-running was held until 1844; this has been the venue of countless markets, military parades, public protests and demonstrations, dances and concerts. In fact, this square is home to some of Pamplona's most important traditional buildings. You can see *Café Iruña* and the *Casino Principal* on the floor above; then there's *La Perla* Hotel where figures as popular and disparate as the Pamplona-born violinist Sarasate and the legendary Ernest Hemingway have stayed; there's also the Palace of Navarre, which is currently the seat of the local government. Previously, the building was used for the administration of the *fueros*, a special charter under which the Navarrese received certain privileges. But more than anything, standing in the square allows you to admire its imperfections and porticoes in their entirety, not forgetting the famous *quiosco* (bandstand) which only dates from 1943, when it replaced a wooden one which, in turn, had originally replaced the famous Mariblanca. This is the real living-room of the city.

From Plaza del Castillo, you can go down Chapitela, where all the grain was brought into the city. This is where Arturo Campión was born, a lawyer, writer and great defender of Basque culture. From here, everything is within a stone's throw. For example, the *churros* (doughnuts) of Calle Mañueta, the street where Pamplona had its first *frontón* (a high wall against which a ball game called *pelota* is played). This *frontón* had so many little nooks and crannies as well as the odd column that the game was really

Luis Paret was commissioned to design some of the city's most important fountains.

hard to control: this is where the local term «*mañuetero*» comes from which refers to a crafty player with all sorts of winning strategies. In fact, it was in Calle Mañueta that a local was born about whom little is known, but who was a maestro of flamenco guitar: Agustín Castellón Campos, known by his stage name «Sabicas». This name derived from his favourite food: broad beans. It is said that he would often repeat «how I'd like to eat a plate of little broad beans (*habicas*) right now!», and from here came his nickname. As we have already mentioned, Calle Mañueta is also famous for its churros shop, the only permanent establishment which makes this highly prized delicacy.

Let's now walk to Navarrería, where in the square, which bears the same name, we can find one of the five neoclassical fountains across Pamplona designed by Luis Paret. The one in Santa Cecilia has acquired unintentional notoriety because in the San Fermín fiestas it has been used as a sort of improvised diving board from which Australians and other nationalities plunge into the air, trusting that their fall will be caught by outstretched arms. However, the absence of the latter has caused more than one serious injury. Nearby we can also see the Rozalejo Palace, a baroque building which was renovated in the 18th century. We can't leave old Navarrería without going to San Fermín de Aldapa church which stands at the heart of what was the original hub of the village. As its name suggests, this church-convent of the Claretians is dedicated to San Fermín and it is from here that the other *sanfermines* originated, the so-called **San Fermín Chiquito,** who gives his name to the fiestas in this neighbourhood of Pamplona which are annually celebrated on September 25. Before visiting the Cathedral, it's worth looking at the Renaissance building which stands at the end of Calle Navarrería: the Institute of Public Administration, if only to admire the Isabellan cloister which is framed and flanked by iron columns. If you are willing to step further into the building, you will come to a back courtyard which looks out onto the Redín, and from where you can see the biggest redwood in Navarre.

You can now visit the 15th century cathedral, the **Catedral de Santa María**, which was built over the ruins of what was a roman temple and, later, a romanesque one. The outside of the cathedral is deceptive, as concealed behind the neoclassical facade designed by Ventura Rodríguez (1783) is a purely gothic interior.

*Pamplona Cathedral.
Façade (left); tomb of
King Carlos III of
Navarre and Queen
Leonor (following
page, top); and aerial
view of the cathedral
and its surroundings
(following page,
bottom).*

The cathedral is dedicated to Santa María La Real, a 12th century romanesque carving which is made
from wood and plated in silver. In the central nave is the mausoleum of Carlos III, the author of the
«Privilege of the Union» treaty in 1423, and his wife, Leonor of Trastamara. Without doubt, the jewel in
the cathedral's crown is the Gothic cloister built between 1286 y 1472 which is one of most beautiful
cloisters in Europe. It boasts 24 pointed arches and five doorways, the most outstanding of which is the
Puerta Preciosa whose decorations narrate the earthly life of the Virgin. Those who want to see more can
visit the Museo Diocesano (Diocesan Museum) or look at the buildings attached to the gothic cathedral
of old Iruña.

The cathedral cloister (opposite page). The Episcopal Palace and its 18th century doorway (above).

There's much more to see but your tour should not neglect a quiet, little square which is nestled under the cathedral's protective wing: Plaza de San José, where on every first Saturday of the month there is a unique little market, referred to as the *mercado de la pulga* (flea market), which sells a weird and wonderful selection of antique objects. This square leads on to two streets: one rather curious street which is blocked at the other end by the convent of the Carmelitas, which the locals ingeniously named «*Salsipuedes*» (Getoutifyoucan); the other street at the far end of the square is Calle Redín which brings us to the city walls which provide an excellent balcony from which to admire the lower neighbourhoods of Rochapea, Chantrea and San Jorge. From this charming corner of the Redín, the old rope-making factory, there is a walk called the **Ronda del obispo Barbazán,** which runs above the city walls and follows the outside and back of the cathedral and its outbuildings until you come to the Episcopal Palace, an 18th century building with a baroque doorway.

We have now come to one of the breaks in the city wall, through which the city expanded to the north, and through which so many pilgrims en route to Santiago de Compostela entered, and still enter, Pamplona. One modern building (1952) is conspicuous due to its high walls and absence of windows. Nicknamed the «*bombonera*» (sweet box), this is the Frontón Labrit located on the hill of the same name. The walls of its court have been hard hit by the world's best pelota players on two occasions. Here, the world pelota championships were held in 1962 and 2002. The Frontón is also used weekly for the most fiercely fought matches in a sport which has been inherited and affectionately sustained by our people: Basque pelota.

Playing Basque pelota (opposite page). Above, one of the bridges over the River Arga.

San Pedro bridge and the River Arga (below).
The Museo de Navarra (Museum of Navarre)
(opposite page).

After going down the Labrit hill a litte way, we soon come to one of the five medieval bridges which cross the river Arga: that of **La Magdalena** which is undoubtedly the most important and elaborate of the five. Its importance derives from the fact that it is the entry point, as we have already said, of the Santiago pilgrimage. The other four bridges are **Puente de San Pedro** which joins Calle del Carmen and the Zumalacárregui gateway with the upper area of the Rochapea neighbourhood; the **Puente de Curtidores**, best known for providing a route for the six bulls which will run the next day in what is known as the «*encierrillo*» (mini bull run), a race which allows the herd to be moved from the *corrales del gas* (bull pens situated on the site of the old gasworks) to the Cuesta de Santo Domingo; the **Puente de Santa Engracia**, situated in Rochapea, a little before the *Cuatro Vientos* junction; and lastly, the **Puente de Miluce** (*Miluze* in the Basque language, *euskera*, means «long tongue») which is home to some of Pamplona's legends such as that of the hanging of the rebels at the order of Carlos II *the Bad.*

Now that we have followed the bridges to almost the outskirts of the city, we need to go back and have another look at the spots that play an important role in the fiestas and which offer us an ideal excuse to see parts of Pamplona which we would otherwise not get to visit.

Without the pressure of running with bulls, and just a few metres from the beginning of the Cuesta de Santo Domingo, we can look at the regional museum, the Museo de Navarra (Museum of Navarre), installed in the building of the old Nuestra Señora de la Misericordia hospital that served as a public hospital until 1925. The facade is still that of the old hospital which was built in 1556 and designed in the plateresque style by Juan de Villarreal. The hospital chapel, dated 1547, is one of the three examples of gothic-renaissance architecture in Pamplona; the two others are the churches of Santo Domingo and San Agustín. Inside the museum, those with limited time should not miss the roman mosaic from Navarre's Villa El Ramalete, the chest of Leire (used for conserving saintly relics) and the portrait painted by Goya, *Marqués de San Adrián* (1804). Ciga, Martín Caro and Oteiza, amongst others, also have noteworthy paintings in this museum, one of the most important museums in Pamplona today.

*Some of the outstanding works on show
at the Museo de Navarra.
On the opposite page, the Marqués
de San Adrián by Goya; on this page,
caliphal marble chest (above), capital
from the Cathedral (left) and detail from
the medieval fresco collection (right).*

Half-way up the Cuesta de Santo Domingo we find the Plaza de Santiago which hosts the Santo Domingo market, Pamplona's oldest, as well as the church-convent of **Santo Domingo,** home to the Pontificia y Real de Santiago University between 1630 and 1771. This building was built in the 16th century under street-level and is notable for its gothic-renaissance interior and its organ with baroque casing from the 17th century, one of the best examples in Navarre. A little further on is the old Seminary of San Juan, where seminarians from the Valley of Baztán were taught. The seminary maintains its early 18th century baroque façade despite a succession of different uses. It has been home to the Carlist Museum and Municipal Archive, a function which it shares today with the Sarasate Museum. Finally, we emerge into the open expanse of the Plaza del Ayuntamiento with a certain sense of relief at leaving such a narrow street behind. We can now relax and admire the façade of the **Ayuntamiento** (Town Hall) in all its splendour. The façade, which dates from 1752, is built in the style of the late baroque in its lower part and early neoclassicism in the upper part. On each floor, the columns are styled according to the three classical orders: Doric, Ionic and Corinthian. Inside the Town Hall you can see a beautiful stained-glass window in the Salón de Plenos which pays tribute to the union of the three *Burgos* (boroughs). You can also admire the seven keys of the city wall which are kept in the Mayor's office, together with the official embroidered flag and the silver maces carried by the macebearers on official occasions. Two stone statues grace the main entrance: *Prudencia* (Prudence) and *Justicia* (Justice).

*Two views of Pamplona's
Town Hall.*

Courtyard of the Cámara de Comptos.

From the Plaza del Ayuntamiento, and although it's deviating from the route somewhat, you shouldn't miss one building, declared a National Monument in 1868 and which, in addition to its intrinsic value, is of powerful symbolic importance. We're talking about the **Cámara de Comptos.** This building was instituted by Carlos II in 1365 to manage the royal family's finances; it was subsequently used as Navarre's Court of Auditors between 1525 and 1836. The medieval building, from the 13th century, is a must-see for anyone visiting Pamplona as it is considered the only example of a gothic civic building in Pamplona. The building's sober exterior is distinguished by the pointed arch of the entrance and small windows, also framed by pointed arches. Step inside and see the attractive internal courtyard and the collection of coins from the different periods of Navarre's history.

*Poteo (drinks) and pinchos (tapas)
in the bars of Pamplona.*

While we're on the subject of identity, we can't possibly leave the *casco viejo* (historic centre) without sparing a thought for the **«poteo»**: a deep-rooted tradition which is maintained even today. Groups of friends meet to have some «*potes*» or glasses of wine, in several of Pamplona's many bars. Traditionally, the venues for the «*poteo*» were three areas in each of the city's three *burgos* (villages): the area of the streets Tejería, Estafeta and Navarrería were the «*poteo*» haunts in Navarrería; the area of Jarauta, also where most of the *peñas* (social clubs which meet to eat, drink and play music) meet during San Fermines, was that used by San Cernin; and people from San Nicolás would congregate in the bars of Calle San Gregorio and San Nicolás. To keep up with the urban expansion, this same ancestral tradition has extended to Pamplona's new neighbourhoods; so, today you can find groups of friends drinking in the neighbourhood of San Juan, Iturrama, and so on. We should point out that it was only the original «*poteo*» that was limited to wine drinking. The tradition has slowly been fleshed out to include the *pincho* or *tapa*. In fact, a whole new culture is growing up around this strange phenomenon in which one mouthful can harbour all the deliciousness of an entire meal. In Pamplona, and other nearby cities, the organisation of special *tapa* or *pincho* weeks has proved particularly popular. Bars compete to win for the prize for the best tapa in town.

River sports.

As a refreshing antidote to the more urban elements of the tour, let's think about the importance that the **River Arga** holds for Pamplona. This river, whose source is in the Quinto Real mountains to the north of Navarre, stretches for 145 kilometres before unloading its waters into the river Aragón outside Funes. The Arga is for Pamplona, if you allow us the comparison, what the Seine is for Paris or the Thames for London. It's the life source that irrigates the fertile region of Magdalena, it's spawned all sorts of sports clubs on its banks (Club Natación, S. D. Amaya, Aranzadi, Lagun Artea, etc.), and it provides fabulous spaces for recreation and walks. In fact, the Arga forms an intrinsic part of life in Pamplona where the locals keep an anxious eye on the water levels which can be very low during dry periods and incredibly high during rainy springs.

On this page, two different views of the Media Luna Park.

From the banks of the Arga we can make our way back towards the natural city wall formed by the way the city plummets down towards the river. From the bastion of San Bartolomé and the exit towards Irún and France, there is a park which, due to its distinctive shape, is called the *Parque de la Media Luna* (Half Moon Park), and which was designed by the Pamplona architect, Víctor Eusa. **Media Luna Park** also provides an excellent spot from which to complete the view which you previously admired from the Redín. Here, you have the entire Chantrea area at our feet as well as the neighbourhoods of Burlada and Villava, and you can see as far as the foothills of the northern Pyrenees. This is a tranquil park with a great variety of ponds, pergolas, benches and cafe terraces to while away the warm summer evenings. Looking over the railings of the viewpoint, on the right you can see to another of the important works by Víctor Eusa in Pamplona: the **San Miguel Seminary**, crowned by an imposing glass and concrete cross which emphasises the building from several points in the city.

Architecture of the Primer Ensanche (First square grid of streets). Buildings on Calle Francisco Bergamin (above) and Calle Jose Alonso (left).

With a tree-filled park and some elegant buildings, Víctor Eusa has been able to make a natural connection between the old walled settlement of Iruña and the new, expanded Pamplona. In the 1930s Pamplona was expanded with a square grid of streets which were formed after the city wall had been knocked down to allow room for the so-called *ensanche* (extension) to become the commercial heart of the city. Built at a later date, and occupying the space outside the first *ensanche*, the second extension – *El Segundo*

Ensanche – is intersected by the Avenida de la Baja Navarra. As we have already said, this extension of Pamplona is characterised by the perfect grid of streets and squares which make up its area. Here, you can see San Francisco Javier church, which was built in the modernist style in 1952, and the market, referred to by the locals as «new», which despite its circular form, looks perfectly at home next to a perfect square block of apartments. At one end of this area stands the impressive monumentality of the enormous *Monumento a los Caídos* (Monument to the Fallen) in the Plaza del Conde Rodezno. Together, the monument and the square provide an iconic landmark for the *Segundo Ensanche* which has acquired the intimate atmosphere of a neighbourhood which sits within the larger structure of the city.

The Segundo Ensanche with its characteristic street grid around the Plaza Blanca de Navarra (below) and the area surrounding the Monumento a los Caídos (right).

*San Cernin church
and its weathercock.*

Pilgrimage route

Pamplona has another string to its bow which makes it an international city: it's «*la primera del Camino*» (the first Spanish city on the Santiago pilgrimage route, in the words of one advertising campaign). The great European pilgrimage to Santiago de Compostela which originated in the 11th century made the path which joined Bordeaux and Astorga – already important to the Romans – an important institution.

The pilgrim route, known as the Camino de Santiago, enters Pamplona via the bridge, Puente de la Magdalena and passes through the borough of Navarrería in front of the Town Hall and enters the borough of San Cernin. The first thing you come across when entering this borough is San Saturnino church, which was built on the site of a roman temple. This temple played an important defensive role when the different boroughs were engaged in internal quarrels. This is why its external structure has retained certain fortress-like elements.

Today, there is still accommodation for pilgrims inside the church which has a host of symbolic features. The weathercock on one of its towers has significance as for many years the cock was the symbol of Pamplona's old savings bank (no longer in existence), the Caja de Ahorros Municipal. Also the «*gallico*» (cock) of San Cernin (the Basque name for Saint Saturnino) is one of the city's most-used emblems, and, for a few years now, has been the symbol of prizes awarded for outstanding achievements by a well-known local *sociedad gastronómica* (private dining club).

Another of the symbols is situated just in front of this church's porticoed vestibule; this is the «*Pocico*» (well), a commemorative plaque on the ground at the junction between the streets Jarauta, Mayor and San Saturnino, which marks the place where, according to tradition, San Saturnino baptized the first Christians including the city's patron saint, Fermín. Another important symbol is the clock tower and the clock itself since every morning it announces the moment when the rocket is fired to announce the start of the bull running. On the site of the ancient cloister, is the chapel of la Virgen del Camino, patron saint of the city who is believed to have appeared on several occasions to locals fighting for possession of the sacred statue made in her image.

From here, the pilgrim route goes up the Calle Mayor, the main road of the old borough of San Cernin and one of the historic centre's main arteries. It is along this street that, on July 6 in the afternoon, all the town hall officials march – wearing their ceremonial outfits and accompanied by their entourage – to San Lorenzo church on the eve of the Saint day dedicated to San Fermín. Young people in traditional festival dress try to bring the procession to a halt by dancing the «Waltz of Astráin» whose chorus has provided the name of the event: «*Riau-Riau*». From 1991 the *riau-riau* has been omitted due to its long duration (up to six hours) and the interference of unruly behaviour. The Calle Mayor is home to several palaces and noble residences, some of which are being renovated. At the beginning of the street, there's the **Palacio del Condestable**, built in 1530, which has served, among other things, as the bishops' residence until 1732, and as a provisional town hall from 1752 to 1760. It was owned by the Duke

Above, San Cernin and the hills beyond. Below, the lintel above the entrance to the Ezpeleta Palace, in Calle Mayor.

of Alba and its internal structure is being knocked down, although the building's future use has yet to be decided. Further on, at number 31, you'll find the **Palacio de Redín y Cruzat,** a large Renaissance house which has been turned into a music school. Undoubtedly, the building of the highest architectural value is the **Palacio de Ezpeleta** situated at number 65. It is the finest baroque construction in Pamplona and its façade bears the scars of a big cannon bolt sent by the Carlists from the Fuerte de San Cristóbal.

*Two views of the
Plaza de Recoletas.
On the opposite page,
San Lorenzo church.*

The Calle Mayor comes out into a square with its own distinctive flavour: the flavour of garlic. In this square, known locally as the la *plaza de los ajos* (the garlic square), walking garlic vendors have over the years come to install themselves here during the bull running. The square takes its real name – Plaza de Recoletas – from the Recoletas nuns whose convent is situated here. The convent was built in 1624 and is a clear example of baroque architecture. Today, the convent church is a highly popular venue for wedding ceremonies.
Practically opposite the Recoletas church-convent is the **Church of San Lorenzo** which, what it might lack in architectural beauty, it more than makes up more in the sentimental value it holds for locals: in the heart of the building is the chapel of San Fermín. This chapel is where all important religious ceremonies are held. What's more, and as is only to be expected, it is the locals' favourite – and for that reason sometimes impossible to secure –, wedding venue. Here, you can look at the statue of San Fermín himself, and you'll be surprised to see how dark skinned he is. But the exact origin of this skin colour remains unknown. One theory is that his image was originally black and another claims that the candles have darkened his image over the years.
After the urban confines of the city appear the Taconera Park and the Santiago pilgrimage route, the Camino de Santiago, which runs along the calle del Bosquecillo to reach and cross the Vuelta del Castillo and its leafy meadow. Then the Camino looses itself in the neighbourhood of Iturrama before coming to the Puerto del Perdón.

*Two sculptures in the Parque de la Ciudadela.
Above, the «Odiseo» by Oteiza; pictured right,
a sculpture by Larrea.
On the following two pages, green spaces
created around the old city fortifications.*

Green spaces

Pamplona has a deserving reputation as one of
the Spanish cities with most parks and trees.
Pamplona is fundamentally green. Green is
the colour of both its flag and its numerous
meadows. While the green of its trees changes
colour according to the time of year, the green
of the vegetable gardens which run along the
banks of the River Arga is constant. Of the 1,896
hectares which make up Pamplona's urban area,
more than 450 of those are gardens or tree-filled
areas. This proportion can compete with the best
of Europe's many attractive cities. Pamplona has
known how to exploit its military fortifications
and create pleasant public spaces, turning them
into places where people can rest, chat, play,
walk or even practise sports. This conversion of
closed, private spaces into open, public ones has
provided the city with real 'lungs' with which
to counter the rising pollution levels of many
nearby cities.
A tour of Pamplona's landscaped parks requires
a greater effort and an almost circular route,
since Pamplona's various parks ring the city in
concentric circles. **El Redín** embraces part of the
city wall and integrates it with the landscape
so it becomes a perfect place from which to
view the city.

Parque de la Taconera. Statues of Julián Gayarre and Mariblanca.
On the opposite page, Media Luna Park and the monument to Sarasate (above)
and Yamaguchi Park (below).

La Taconera is another garden which is landscaped in the French style and also acts as a viewing point for the lower part of Rochapea, mount San Cristóbal and the north-western outskirts of Pamplona. The **Vuelta del Castillo** is a real green 'lung' within the city; the English refinement of the setting provides most of the population with somewhere pleasant to relax. With the Ciudadela nearby, it is also the perfect place for civil weddings, firework celebrations and football matches amongst friends. The **Media Luna** is another of Pamplona's great viewpoints, although this time it sits atop a natural city wall which descends almost vertically to the River Arga.

This first circle gives way to a bigger one: **Yamaguchi,** a Japanese-style garden which was designed by gardeners from the twin city of Yamaguchi. It is a combination of an English park with abundant green spaces and an oriental garden. Close to this park and almost hidden from view is the Planetarium, an absolute gem which screens astronomy projections as well as all sorts of interesting exhibitions; it also boasts a lecture theatre, exhibition gallery and circular film theatre.

Two views of Yamaguchi Park.

The Planetarium, from the outside (above) and inside (below).

*Campus of Navarre's
Universidad Pública.*

The two **University Campuses** are another green
space which provide sound insulation from
the noise and smoke of the city and create the
tranquil atmosphere necessary for study and
research. We can consider **Soto de Lezkairu**
a natural park which was created out of the
necessity to provide a residential area with
somewhere to relax, play and practise sports.
The still-incomplete **Fluvial del Arga Park** is
the biggest of the parks as it follows the river's
course across the city and even the surrounding
region. It's a real luxury to be able to stroll
along the bank of the Arga which, unlike many
rivers, is blessed with a course which is not
tortuously winding. Numerous benches and
lamps line this walk which is frequented daily by
hundreds of locals. The **Parque del Mundo** has
the curious claim of standing where what was
known as the old *manicomio* (insane asylum)
stood, that is before it was later referred to as
the psychiatric hospital. The Town Hall wanted
to give it a sophisticated touch and so tree and
shrub species from different parts of the world
were planted, hence the park's title. Finally,
Biurdana Park completes the biggest circle we
have traced around the city. This park runs along
the left margin of the river where it runs close
to San Jorge. It's a green space which those who
live nearby use as a place to meet and relax,
especially during the fiesta season because of the
smoke which envelops the celebrations. These
are just some of the places which Pamplona's
residents frequent in their leisure time.

*The River Sadar which runs through
the university campus.*

Outside the city, we can also enjoy the **Sierra
del Perdón Natural Park** which is 20 km
outside Pamplona and whose south side sits
on the limits of the Pamplona region.
Twenty-five kilometres to the north of the city
is **Valle de la Ulzama,** referred to as Navarre's
own Switzerland, which is home to a special
protected area known as the **Robledal de
Orgi** where there are unique examples of
Pedunculate oaks – the Latin term for the old
English oak tree.
We may have omitted to mention some of the
more recent additions to this green inventory,
but it is obviously not possible in this short
guidebook to give an exhaustive list of all
Pamplona's green spaces. We'll leave it to you
to discover or chance upon any other parks
for yourself.

PROXIMITY AND MODERNITY

Like many cities of its size, Pamplona has a real network of nearby communities which, to a more or lesser extent, have become a residential commuter belt for those who work in the city. Some, however, have been keen to conserve their identity as villages in their own right. In our definition of nearby areas (which are mostly situated along the course of the River Arga), we are talking about those which lie in the river basin. Someone defined «the real river basin» as those areas from which you can hear the cathedral bells. This same idea can be used to describe a small circle around Pamplona, whose radius does not for the most part exceed 10 km.

The casa-taller (house-studio) of the sculptor, Jorge Oteiza.

In **Gazólaz,** a village situated 7 km southwest of Pamplona, there is a beautiful example of a Romanesque porticoed church. Walking into the small village square is like coming upon a haven of peace and tranquillity, and the church and its porticoed vestibule transport the visitor to medieval times. On the opposite side of Pamplona, but still situated in the river basin, you can visit another small village – **Alzuza** – which just 8 km away from Pamplona is home to a cultural gem: the **House-studio of Jorge Oteiza**. This sculptor was born in Orico, was awarded the prestigious *Príncipe de Asturias* arts prize, and lived for many years in this village close to Pamplona. This unique building, which arguably detracts your attention from the original house a little too much, was designed by the architect Sáez de Oiza. Inside, there are three distinct spaces you can visit.

A space inside the house-studio of Jorge Oteiza.

El Laboratorio (The Laboratory) traces the artist's creative process – from his tools and materials to the resulting sculptures. Then there's *la Casa* (House), the space which invites the visitor into the artist's way of seeing. Together, manuscripts, objects and texts, and the artist's office, conceived as a workplace, offer an excellent insight into the artist's personality. Finally, there's *el Taller* (the studio). Educational activities are held in this space which is not open to visitors like the laboratory and house. Open from Tuesday to Friday, 10am to 3pm, and on Saturdays, Sundays and bank holidays, 11am to 7pm, Oteiza's house/workshop hosts temporary exhibitions, discussion groups and an excellent permanent collection of works by the artist. To proximity, we have added modernity since, in the last few years, Pamplona has acquired a host of new architect-designed buildings. But as to whether these constructions are successful and well conceived, only time will tell.

In the geographic centre of Pamplona and boasting a new wing which puts it amongst Spain's premier buildings, is the highly popular **Baluarte**, the conference centre and auditorium designed by the Navarre architect, Patxi Mangado. Its L-shape arrangement creates a large public square measuring 10.000 m². This square together with the versatility of the building's internal spaces – the centre can host conferences and shows of different sizes –, and its privileged position next to the Ciudadela Park, means that Pamplona is more than well equipped to host any important cultural event.

Pictured above and on the following two pages: two views of the Baluarte Convention Centre.

Above and opposite, Navarre's Royal and General Archives building, designed by Rafael Moneo.

In the heart of Iruña oldtwown, next to San Fermín de Aldapa, there is another majestic modern building which brings together old and new. The **Royal and General Archives** building by the Navarre architect Rafael Moneo has converted the old palace of the viceroys into a landmark building which rises up above the River Arga and whose stone façade radiates a sun-kissed glow. This is one of the most emblematic projects by the

internationally renowned architect and deserves a visit – both of its practical interior and impressive exterior.
We feel confident that our modernity will continue to be intimately linked with the conversation of our most beautiful old buildings.

Left-hand page, Pamplona's patron saint, San Fermín. Above, the procession dedicated to the saint which is held every July 7. On the following two pages, the encierro (bull run).

FIESTA

Whether we like it or not, the concept of *fiesta* is inseparable from life in Pamplona. Although some locals may feel that our fiesta gets talked about far too much, the fact remains that no tour of the city would be complete without a look at the important spots which, for seven days a year, are at the heart of our world famous fiesta. There is, without doubt, one San Fermines ritual *par excellence*. Others may hold a more intimate importance for some locals, but the most original and internationally intriguing ritual which, every morning of the week-long fiesta, keeps everyone in suspense, is none other than the **bull running**, or *encierro*. The word *encierro* has more resonance and associations for those of us from Pamplona than any other Spanish speaker could possibly imagine. The bull-running is unique; it's the only part of our fiesta which is shown in five continents across the world.

*Three different aspects
of the bull running.*

We should first go back to what precedes the
bull run; by this I don't mean historically, but
rather what happens the day before each of the
bull runs, which can be followed so minutely on
TV. We have to go down to the neighbourhood
of Rochapea, one of Pamplona's oldest and most
traditional areas. Just after crossing the Puente
de Curtidores (Tanners' Bridge), one of the city's
medieval bridges we mentioned earlier, we come
to the so-called *Corrales del gas* (bull pens on
the site of the old gasworks) on the left. In 1861,
according to Doctor Arazuri – the author of a
book about the streets of Pamplona-Iruña –
a gasworks was set up for public lighting and
domestic use. The gas reached the city via a
network of pipes, and houses were fitted with gas
meters. One of the latter can still be seen in the
Palace of the Counts of Guenduláin, in Plaza del
Consejo. As well as gas, the factory sold carbon
fuel, tar, coal tar, ammonia water, fireproof oven
bricks, limestone and lead piping.
During the Second Carlist War, the gasworks was
forced to shut due to a lack of raw materials.
It remained abandoned until in 1899 it was
used by the Town Hall, – first provisionally and

later with the addition of a small building –, as somewhere to unload and keep the bulls (which came from herds in Castile and Andalusia) before they ran and fought in the fiestas. It is still here that all the bulls which are due to participate in San Fermines await the so-called *encierrillo*: a little-known event which takes place every evening during the fiesta and consists in taking those bulls, which are due to take part the next day in the bull running, held in the morning, and the bullfights, held in the afternoon, to the corrals or pens in Santo Domingo.

On Santo Domingo hill, which appears every morning on televisions around the world, you can see the little vaulted niche where young locals pray to the Saint for his protection just a few minutes before the bull running begins. So at 7:55, 7:57 and 7:59am, you can hear the well-known words which, translated into English, go like this:

> «*To San Fermín we ask*
> *that as our patron*
> *he guides us in the bull run*
> *and gives us his blessing*»

Then the bull runners shout «Viva San Fermín, Gora San Fermín» (Long live San Fermín). This same ritual is repeated every morning. This hill which barely stretches 280 metres from the pens to the Plaza del Ayuntamiento, is one of the most difficult parts of the course due to the power and speed with which the bulls run along its length. Following the course of the bull run, we come to a short street, Calle de Mercaderes, which widens into Calle Estafeta, home to the notoriously dangerous bend – *la curva de Estafeta* – where every year the bulls charge against the protective barrier. The entire length of Calle Estafeta is on a downward slope, with few refuge points for the runners. It is on the last part of this street that the bulls can become easily distracted or fall behind – both situations are potentially dangerous.

After the end of Calle Estafeta, there are just the 100 metres of the Telefónica stretch which, with its downward slope, slows the pace and prepares

A sea of red and white figures surges along the streets during the fiestas.

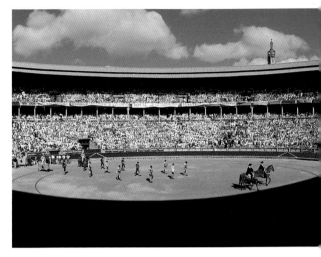

*Pamplona's bullring and the notorious
social division of its tendidos (stands).*

the bulls for the final bottleneck of the Callejón
(alley), where human pile-ups can occur due to
the domino effect of one runner falling down. In
the bull run's long history, there have been a total
of 24 «pile-ups» which have caused more than
700 injured victims and miraculously, although
regrettably, only a couple of deaths.

There are all sorts of fascinating figures and
statistics attached to the bull running, and
although this is not the ideal place to list them in
any detail, we will nonetheless offer a few: the
course is 848,6 metres long; its average duration
is 3 minutes and 55 seconds; and the average
speed of the bulls is 24 kilometres per hour.

The longest-ever bull run was on July 11, 1959
when a *Miura* bull fell behind and because it
refused to enter the pen in the square, a sheepdog
had to egg it on and bite its legs until it agreed to
enter the pen.

The average number of bull runners who are
injured is between 200 and 300 each year.

According to our records, the total number of
runners speared and injured by the bull's horns
is 215 and there has been a total of 13 deaths in
the bull run's history.

But there is more to the fiesta of San Fermín
than bulls, and so we would like, albeit briefly,
to look at some other aspects of Pamplona's
most important fiesta. There is one element
which has become less important with time,
especially since the fiesta has been attended
by an ever-increasing number of people: the
«*Peñas*» (organised social clubs) which used
to be at the very centre of the fiesta's nightlife.
Social change, difficulties in finding party
venues and people moving away are amongst
the many reasons for the reduced popularity
of the «*Peñas*». Not forgetting, of course, the
political aspect of these famous social groups.
Established in 1903, «*La Única*» (The Only
One) holds the claim to being the first such
group, or *peña*, to be established, hence its
name. In the 1950s, *peñas* were set up around
organisations, sports or arts clubs, and so on. In
some cases, the process took the reverse form
and from an existing *peña*, a sports, culture
or leisure club was set up. To many people,
even foreigners, these are just some of the
peña names that are familiar: Aldapa, Alegría
de Iruña, Anaitasuna, El Bullicio, La Jarana,
Oberena, etc. Almost all of them have been set
up from dining clubs which put their sign out
at fiesta-time and go to the bull running and
bullfights as an excuse for a good time. Some
are simply fun-seeking and others original or

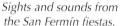

*Sights and sounds from
the San Fermín fiestas.*

even indifferent. Pamplona's bullring, unlike any other, dare we say, in the world, is divided into two radically different, and sometimes opposing, parts. The sun marks an invisible wall which places a vast divide between those who occupy one side of the ring (*la sombra*, or shade) and those who occupy the other (*el sol*, or sun). The shady side is «Lidia» (the bullfight in all its splendour), silence, those who are experts in bullfights, and others who pretend to be experts, champagne, seafood and maybe a delicate sandwich... Meanwhile, the sun-filled camp is like organised anarchy. The sunny side is all about big filling sandwiches wrapped in aluminium foil, dustbins filled with sangria, flour, eggs and any other throwable objects. The bullfight proceeds according to the skill of the bullfighter, and in the space of minutes the emotions in the stands can go from utter respect and adoration to the fiercest disapproval. It's the eternal conflict between north and south, rich and poor, the well-to-do and the plebeian...

If you were to spend the entire day at the fiesta of Sanfermines, the day wouldn't be complete without hearing the trumpet call of the reveille sounded throughout the city, witnessing the world famous bull running and after that, indulging in a hearty breakfast of hot chocolate with *churros* (long doughnut sticks) to fortify you for the rest of the day. After breakfast, you can go to the «Baile de la alpargata» (Espadrille Dance) in the Casino Principal and then follow the carnival giants with their enormous heads around the streets and squares to the sound of the bagpipes and the drums. The *Gigantes* of Pamplona go back more than 100 years, as there is evidence to prove that in 1860, the Town Hall paid the master painter Tadeo Amorena a sum of 3,600 copper and silver reales (coins) to build two new giants to represent Europe. In the same year, he was also commissioned to make another six new giants to represent the world's other continents, for the sum of 6,000 reales.

Below, Pamplona's carnival Gigantes (Giants), famous around the world. Opposite page, more images of the celebrations.

These new giants were to substitute others which the cathedral committee had given to the Town Hall in 1839; in fact, there is written evidence from the 16th century that the giants danced and accompanied the cathedral committee ahead of the procession. The giants also played an important part in all the big celebrations held in the 20th century, and in 1965 they travelled to New York, where they towered over the city rather like its tall buildings.

Between 11 am and 1pm, we can choose between a number of taurine shows, folk music or dancing, rural sports or any number of games or entertainment. At 1pm we should go to the «*Apartado*», which is when the line-up of bulls is decided for each bullfighter. This event, which elsewhere has often been a private event, has become a social occasion in Pamplona that is attended by the «beautiful» people so they can see themselves in the newspaper the next day.

At this time of day it's best to stop off and have one, or several, aperitifs, according to how many you can manage. If you like, you can also go the Club Taurino and attend a meeting about the bulls due to fight the same afternoon. At lunchtime, you definitely need to sit down and eat in order to get your strength up; in fact, you've got until 5.30pm to do so. But you shouldn't miss the *paseo de las mulillas* (procession of the mules) on the way to the bullring. At six o'clock, you should make your way to the bullfight, that is if you've been lucky enough to get your hands on a ticket. If not, Pamplona offers a host of entertainment and music in any of its numerous squares. In the early evening, you could go and listen to the flute players and drummers, or take a stroll through the fairground where, according to the state of your stomach, you can also grab a bite to eat. At 11pm, the crowd-pulling fireworks ceremony kicks off, and is enjoyed by all generations alike. The night is still young and there's a host of open-air dances – both public and private – which provide the best way of staying on your feet until half past six in the morning. All you can do is warm up with a hot drink and... keep on going!

Pamplona combines progress and quality of life, without forgetting to commemorate its famous ambassadors.

BALANCE

There are many more things to see in Pamplona, but we couldn't possibly list everything here. But finally we'd like to say a word about the equilibrium of this city which successfully, and almost effortlessly, seems to create a harmonious balance between history and modernity: in a few steps, and almost without noticing, you can go from the old city walls of the park to the rectilinear street grid of modern Pamplona. The city does not neglect its industrial life but has created industrial estates around its dominant, perhaps too dominant, car industry; it is also working towards 'greener' industries which use more economic fuels. In fact, Pamplona is something of a pioneer when it comes to ecology: it has pioneered a program for the recycling of certain domestic waste materials and is ecological in its use of water. The city has a water purification network so that it can exploit the water from its river for sports and leisure facilities. Pamplona balances its present identity with that of old Iruña and Roman Pompaelo with the same nobility with which its carnival giants dance during the fiestas. It is a city which is always

accessed from below and which always sits on high, enveloped by its city walls. But whatever the time of year, and regardless of whether its trees are green, ochre or bare, Pamplona always offers a warm welcome to any visitor. While we're on the subject of balance, we should also take a look at the valuable contributions that Pamplona has received from the figures whose statutes, buildings and artworks which, in one way or another, have left their indelible mark on the streets and parks. There's Sáenz de Oiza who impressed all with his plans for a public university; José María Escrivá who set up the Opus Dei University in Pamplona; Oteiza, who has bequeathed the city more than 50 sculptures, parks and public spaces; Ignacio Baleztena who was the folk-loving founder of the Muthiko *peña*, the man behind the Riau-Riau chorus and the author of the famous *Uno de enero* (January 1); Pablo Sarasate who was a violinist and composer without par; Rafael Moneo and his Royal and General Archives building; Ernest Hemingway who promoted our fiestas in the English-speaking world; Víctor Eusa whom we mentioned earlier; Remigio Múgica the founder of the Orfeón Pamplonés (choral society); the cyclist Miguel Indurain, who, even though not from Pamplona, helped put Pamplona on televisions all over the world; Manuel Turrillas, who brought music to the fiestas and wrote many of the hymns sung by the Sanfermines *peñas*; José M. Pérez de Salazar, the man who introduced the «*chupinazo*» – the firing of a rocket to signal the start of the bull run; the film-maker Montxo Armendáriz; and Doctor Arazuri who left invaluable visual documents of the city. And so many others, too numerous to name.

All that remains for us to do is to quote the words which appear on the lintel above the Town Hall's main entrance:

«Patet ómnibus jauna, cor valde magis»
The door is open to everyone, but above all our heart.